Indian Tales
A BAREFOOT COLLECTION

written by Shenaaz Nanji

illustrated by Christopher Corr

Barefoot Books
Celebrating Art and Story

All over India, stories are a part of daily life. The best-known stories have been passed by word of mouth (the 'oral tradition') from one generation to the next. Professional storytellers travel from one district to the next, earning their living through their performances. Stories are also told through folk songs, dances, plays and puppet shows, as well as through elaborate murals decorating the walls of temples and other ancient buildings.

The stories you will find in this book each come from a different region in India, from Punjab in the north to Tamil Nadu in the south. I hope that you will have lots of fun as you journey through them, and that they will give you a special taste of the magical land that is India.

Shenaaz Nanji, 2007

Contents

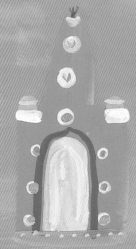

Welcome to India!

Welcome to India! You have entered a land that is overflowing with colours and contrasts and teeming with life. India is the seventh largest country in the world, and its population of over a billion people is second only in size to that of China. Stretching from the majestic Himalayan mountains of the north to the tropical peninsula of the south, it offers a dazzling variety of languages, landscapes, customs, beliefs and lifestyles. This is a country where old and new come together as nowhere else on earth, and you can't help but notice it!

Here, old is very old indeed. Prehistoric sites in India date back to many thousands of years BC. The Indus Valley civilisation flourished in the north-west between 2600 and 1500 BC and was one of the first urban cultures in the world. Its major cities were Harappa and Mohenjo-Daro. Later, the Vedic age (1500–600 BC) saw the development of Sanskrit writing, one of the oldest scripts in the world. During this period, the ancient Vedas were recorded. These texts include hymns, prayers, rituals, chants and even magic spells. Together with the great epics that followed, these texts shaped the understanding of life that we know as Hinduism, India's most widespread religion. The great epic the 'Mahabharata' (from which the story 'Damayanti and Nala' comes) was composed during this period, and the 'Ramayana' (the source for 'Hanuman's Adventures') also has ancient origins.

In later centuries, many dynasties rose and fell. India is rich in resources, so trade both within and beyond its borders has always flourished, and influences from overseas as well as inland have shaped the art and culture of different eras. Of these influences, the arrival of Islam — first through Arab traders in the 7th century and then through the Mughals in the 16th century — has had a huge and lasting impact on art, literature and society.

Today, India is a thriving modern country where all kinds of customs, beliefs, traditions and art forms continue to flourish alongside each other. It is a place where you will find ancient temples and elegant mosques, bustling bazaars, overcrowded buses, imposing tombs and forts, and a dizzying array of scents, spices and aromas. At the same time, you cannot help but be aware that India is changing rapidly — skyscrapers are a feature in every major city, and modern technology has drastically altered many people's lives. But much remains the same: there may be many differences between the numerous regions and peoples of this land, yet underlying all of them is a special, enduring quality that makes India unique.

CHINA
JAMMU and KASHMIR
HIMALAYAS
INDUS
PUNJAB
TIBET
PAKISTAN
HARYANA
ARUNACHAL PRADESH
BRAHMAPUTRA
NEPAL
BHUTAN
DELHI
THAR DESERT
UTTAR PRADESH
SIKKIM
ASSAM
BIHAR
MEGHALAYA
RAJASTHAN
GANGES
BANGLADESH
TRIPURA
MIZORAM
MADHYA PRADESH
INDIA
HOOGHLY
WEST BENGAL
CALCUTTA
GUJARAT
NARMAD
GODAVARI
ORISSA
MUMBAI
ARABIAN SEA
MAHARASHTRA
DECCAN PLATEAU
HYDERABAD
EASTERN GHATS
BAY of BENGAL
KARNATAKA
GOA
WESTERN GHATS
ANDHRA PRADESH
CHENNAI
KAVERI
KERALA
TAMIL NADU
INDIAN OCEAN

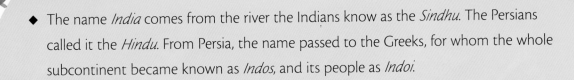

- The name *India* comes from the river the Indians know as the *Sindhu*. The Persians called it the *Hindu*. From Persia, the name passed to the Greeks, for whom the whole subcontinent became known as *Indos*, and its people as *Indoi*.

- India is bordered by the majestic Himalayan mountains in the north, the Arabian Sea to the west, the Bay of Bengal to the east and the Indian Ocean to the south.

- Over a billion people live in India, speaking 23 major languages (including Hindi and English), and 1,500 other languages and dialects.

- The largest cities in India are Delhi and Calcutta in the north and Mumbai (formerly Bombay) and Chennai (formerly Madras) in the south.

- The Deccan Plateau is covered with black volcanic soil and ancient crystalline rocks. Gold, diamonds and other minerals are mined here.

- The hills of the Western and Eastern Ghats are covered with forests of teak, rosewood and sandalwood. Many orchid species also grow here.

- Asian elephants are now an endangered species — there are only 45,000, compared to about 250,000 African elephants.

- There are even fewer tigers than elephants in India — maybe as few as 3,000. They live in the foothills of the Himalayas, the mangrove forests of the Suderbans in Bengal, the forests of Rajasthan and the jungles of Madhya Pradesh in central India.

- The king cobra, which is the largest poisonous snake in the world, lives in India.

- The monsoon season brings torrential rain, floods and even cyclones to India. The south-west monsoon starts in Kerala from June to August. The north-east monsoon starts in Bengal bringing rain from September to December.

GUJARAT

Gujarat lies on the west coast of India. This state has fascinating archaeological sites, amazing architecture, rare wildlife and remarkable people.

Gujarat's people celebrate nearly two thousand festivals and holidays every year! A famous festival is Navaratri, the nine-day Hindu festival that is mentioned in 'The Drummer Boy' and which celebrates the 'Divine Shakti' or the mother-goddess who supports the entire universe. During the festival, people fast all day and dance all night long. Ghopal, the drummer boy, remembers in particular the drums played at the garba dance, during which women sing and clap while going round a statue of Ambaji, goddess of might and power.

In Gujarat, henna tattooing is part of the Adivasi or tribal women's wedding traditions, as seen in this story. Intricate designs are painted on the bride's face and arms. The henna ceremony is considered so sacred in some religions that unless the mother-in-law has applied the first dot of henna to the bride's hand, the painting — and indeed the whole wedding — cannot go ahead.

◆ The dances performed during Navaratri are unique. Raas, for example, is a very energetic dance in which men and women dance in pairs holding sticks called dandiya.

◆ Divaali is a four-day festival that marks the Hindu New Year. It is known as the 'Festival of Lights'.

◆ Janmashtami is a holiday in honour of Lord Vishnu, known as the god of all Hindu gods. Jagat Mandir, a 1,400-year-old temple in the sacred town of Dwarka, is the main place for celebration.

◆ Holi, the celebration of colours, is another important Hindu festival. Bonfires are lit on the night of the full moon, celebrating the end of winter.

◆ Gujarat is a vegetarian state. During celebrations, an Indian meal called thali is served in small steel bowls on a round silver platter. Typical dishes include different curries, rice, bread or roti, curd, chutney or pickles, and a sweet dish. Favourite ingredients include yoghurt, buttermilk, coconut, groundnut, sesame seeds, chutney and pickles.

The Drummer Boy

There once lived a young boy called Ghopal, with big, kind eyes that lit up when he smiled. He lived with his mother in a small hut in a village in Gujarat. Ever since he had seen the drummers play at garba during the festival of Navaratri, he really, really wanted a drum.

Every day, Ghopal woke up before sunrise and hurried to finish his chores. He gathered dung from the cowshed next to their hut, shaped it into patties and spread them out to dry. Later, he would collect the patties in a basket and carry it to the stove in the corner of the yard where Ma cooked.

10

Ma made a living by pounding flour for the shopkeepers who then sold it in little packets at their shops. As she ground the grain in the mortar, Ghopal was transformed into the drummer boy. He sat on the mud floor, placed the tin pot upside down on his lap, and tapped his fingers on it. He could play any sound. He played the sounds of the earth shaking, the ocean lashing and the wind clashing. And as he played, he sang:

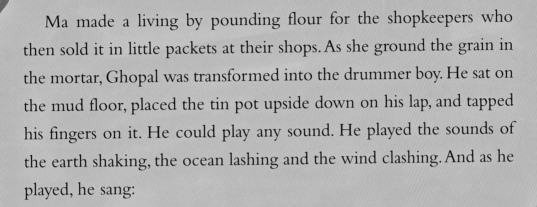

'If I had a drum, a big drum, a big bass drum,
My heart would boom, boom, boom.
Tak dhama dhoom dhoom dhoom!'

'Gho-pal, Gho-pal, Gho-pal!' his mother cried, to remind him to get on with his other chores.

At the third cry, he would rise.

When he milked the buffalo, the drumbeats played in his head. *Tak dhama dhoom dhoom dhoom!* When he went to fetch the water, the drumbeats played all the way to the village well. *Tak dhama dhoom dhoom dhoom!* At night when all was still, the drumbeats played. *Tak dhama dhoom dhoom dhoom!*

GUJARAT

One day, Ghopal saw that his mother's face was cheery and decided it was a good time to ask.

'Ma, I want to buy a drum.'

'A drum?' Ma's brows rose. 'What will you do with a drum?' she asked. 'A drum will not fill your stomach.' She tweaked his nose playfully.

Ghopal nibbled his lower lip. How could he describe the flip-flop flutters he felt when he heard the sound of drums? How could he explain the magic of the boom-boom beats that tingled in his fingers? It was his heart that he wanted to satisfy, not his stomach. He forced a smile, not wishing to upset his mother.

She patted him on the head. 'Look, I've a lot of left-over flour today,' she said. 'I will make some hot-hot pakoras for you.' She skinned and sliced a few potatoes, onions and aubergines into rings and dipped them into the batter of flour. Then she slipped them into the sizzling oil in the frying pan.

The smell of spicy pakoras drifted into his nostrils. Ghopal loved the crispy golden fritters, but

12

he ate only a few. He was too busy thinking up a plan. He wrapped up the rest of the pakoras in a cloth and slipped them into his pocket. Soon he would have his very own drum.

He set off for the market. On the way, he came upon a potter lady with a crying child strapped on her back. He felt sorry for the little boy. 'Are you hungry?' he asked, and brought out the pakoras from his pocket. 'Here, have some.'

The little boy stopped crying and began to eat. Ghopal folded the cloth round the remaining pakoras and slipped them back into his pocket. There were still plenty left over for his plan.

'You are very kind,' said the potter lady to Ghopal, kissing the back of his hand. 'I can't pay you as I have not sold any of my wares. Will you please accept a pot instead?'

A clay pot was not what Ghopal wanted, but he had a satisfying feeling in his heart as the hungry boy smiled at him through his tears. He thanked the lady and went on his way. He had a long way to go

to reach the market. Strumming his fingers on the pot, he made his way along, singing:

'If I had a drum, a big drum, a big bass drum,
My heart would boom, boom, boom.
Tak dhama dhoom dhoom dhoom!'

Soon the sun shone fiercely and his throat felt dry like the cracked mud track. He was glad he had a pot, and stopped at a gurgling stream to scoop up some water for drinking.

As he was filling his pot, he saw an angry man yelling at his wife. 'You broke the pot!'

'I slipped. I'm sorry, I didn't mean to break it,' the poor washerwoman sobbed into her hands. At her feet lay the shattered shards of the clay pot.

'What will we do now? How will we collect water?' The husband shook his angry fist at his frightened wife.

Ghopal felt sorry for her. Quickly, he drank the water from his pot and went to the washerwoman. 'You can have my pot. I don't need it anymore.' He gave it to her.

The washerwoman looked at Ghopal in disbelief. 'I like your big kind eyes.' She took off her shawl from her shoulders and held it out. 'Bless your heart, beta. Please take this as payment for your pot.'

GUJARAT

It was a bright shawl knitted with many different colours of wool. A shawl was not what Ghopal wanted, but he accepted it politely and thanked her. Hanging it round his neck, he took off, singing:

'*If I had a drum, a big drum, a big bass drum,*
My heart would boom, boom, boom.
Tak dhama dhoom dhoom dhoom!'

Soon he passed by a rich merchant on a white stallion. Catching sight of Ghopal's shawl, the merchant came to a halt.

'Young boy, from where did you buy that beautiful shawl?' he asked. 'It is exactly the kind my sick wife would love. I have just bought a dozen shawls for her at the market, but none of them are as pretty as yours.'

Ghopal imagined the merchant's sick wife lying in bed in pain and felt sorry for her. He said a washerwoman had given him the shawl and that she had probably knitted it. 'Sir, give my shawl to your wife.' He took it off and gave it to the merchant.

'Bless you, kind boy.' The surprised merchant thanked Ghopal dearly. 'Will you please take my horse as payment for your shawl?'

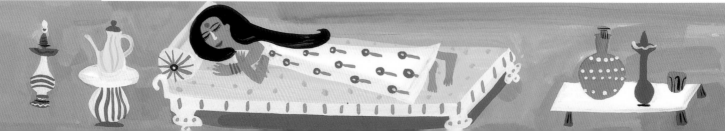

THE DRUMMER BOY

Now a horse was not what Ghopal wanted, but he nodded and accepted it. He mounted the white horse, sat on the red velvet saddle and rode away, singing:

'If I had a drum, a big drum, a big bass drum,
My heart would boom, boom, boom.
Tak dhama dhoom dhoom dhoom!'

Just up the road, in a shady patch beneath some lemon trees, he saw a bustling crowd gathered under a shimiana, a bright red awning raised on four bamboo poles. A wedding party! He was eager to see the bride.

As he drew closer, he took in the strong smells of camphor and burning sandalwood. The beautiful bride sat in a bright red sari adorned with garlands of marigolds. A gold tikka, or ornament, crowned her forehead. Her wrists were covered with bangles and her hands and feet painted with intricate henna designs. A small sacred fire burned in a corner where the bride and groom would circle round and take vows to proclaim their love and respect for each other. Dancers acted out stories and the musicians

played many instruments, but Ghopal's gaze was glued to the drums. His heart ached for a drum.

Suddenly, a priest in a long saffron robe rose to address the audience. 'The groom is delayed. The position of the stars will change! We will have to cancel this wedding.'

The bride began to cry. Whispering broke out among the guests. 'What will we do?' The drummers stopped playing the drums.

'Wait,' cried Ghopal. Heads turned to stare at him. 'This wedding will go on,' he said. 'I will fetch the groom.' He asked where the young man lived and galloped away on his horse at the speed of light.

Very soon, he returned on his horse with the groom behind him. The bride was delighted. 'Kind boy, how can I repay you? Is there anything you want?' she asked.

'A drum,' Ghopal said at once, and his heart went *boom*.

The bride smiled. 'We have many, many drums,' she said. She told the musicians to bring their drums over at once.

There were big drums and small drums, hard drums and soft drums, drums of every colour. She looked at Ghopal. 'You can pick whichever drum you like.'

Ghopal's eyes lit up. He chose a big bass drum that was as blue as the sky. He thanked the bride, mounted his horse and away he went to the market, jigglety-jolt, jigglety-jolt, thinking he was the luckiest boy in the whole world. And he still had the pakoras in his pocket.

THE DRUMMER BOY

He would go on with his plan to sell them at the market. Now that he had his drum, he would give the money to Ma.

The market teemed with people selling all sorts of goods. It was noisy and smelly. Wasps and flies buzzed. Ghopal cried, 'Pakoras for sale! Pakoras for sale!'

Nobody heard him. His voice was lost in the hustle and bustle. He slunk into a corner. How would he attract people's attention? He began to play his drum. He alternated with his right and left hand, playing faster and faster. *Tak dhama dhoom dhoom dhoom!*

The beats were hypnotic and attracted a large crowd. People began to sing and dance. Soon all of his pakoras were sold.

'Mmmmm. Very tasty,' said the people as they ate them.

A man in a gold-embroidered kurta came by. 'How much is that drum, young boy?'

'Sorry, sahib,' said Ghopal. 'My drum's not for sale.' He would never part with his drum.

At the end of the day, he counted his clinking coins. He could hardly wait to see Ma's happy face. He took his drum and got on his horse, singing all the way home:

'I have a drum, a big drum, a big blue, bass drum.
And my heart goes boom, boom, boom.
Tak dhama dhoom dhoom dhoom!
Tak dhama dhoom dhoom dhoom!'

PUNJAB

Punjab is in the heart of the Indus Valley of northern India. The traditional dress for Punjabi men is the salwar kurta, baggy trousers with a long, loose shirt. The women wear salwar kameez. The salwar are long trousers and the kameez is a long tunic, accented by a scarf called a chunni or dupatta — as worn by Bopuluchi's friends in this story. Sometimes they wear a sari — a length of cloth wrapped around the skirt, draped over the blouse on the shoulder, and often pulled up to cover their heads, just like Bopuluchi does at her wedding. The sherwani, worn by her bridegroom, is a long, coat-like garment, buttoned at the front and usually embroidered or decorated.

When a young Punjabi marries, one of the most important rituals is the chuda or bangle ceremony, where the maternal uncle (like the pretend 'uncle' or mama-ji in this story) presents the bride-to-be with a set of white and red bangles called chuda (white denotes purity and red signifies wealth and fertility). This ceremony confirms that a suitable match for his niece has been found.

◆ Punjab was one of the centres of the prehistoric Indus Valley civilisation — the earliest civilisation in India.

◆ Bhangra, the dance that features at Bopuluchi's wedding, originated in Punjab and has developed into a form of popular music.

◆ Wheat is the main starch in the Punjabi diet — many people eat rice only on special occasions. The breads are baked in tandoors, which are ovens that are half buried in the ground with hot coals placed underneath.

◆ A popular Punjabi desert that Bopuluchi makes is kheer, a sweet dish made of milk, rice and sugar. Jalebi, which the robber brings, is a sweet orange pretzel served at special occasions like birthdays and weddings.

◆ After a Punjabi wedding, the bride celebrates leaving her parents' house by throwing phulian, or puffed rice, over her head. This symbolises her good wishes for her parents in their future life.

Bopuluchi

There once was a brave girl, Bopuluchi, who lived alone in a hut on the hilly tracts of Punjab in the far north of India.

Every day, Bopuluchi went with her friends to draw water from the well. One morning, a robber hid near the well, watching the girls, the ends of their bright dupattas flying in the breeze like wings.

While filling their pots with water, the girls talked about their dreams and desires.

'I will marry a rich raja's son,' said one.

'I will marry a skilled archer like Arjuna,' said another friend.

'And I will marry a valiant warrior as invincible as Lord Indra,' said another.

Bopuluchi, the prettiest of them all, was quiet. Her parents had died when she was very young. She had no one to pay her dowry or arrange her marriage.

'What will you do?' the girls asked Bopuluchi.

She looked down. 'I hope the gods send someone for me.'

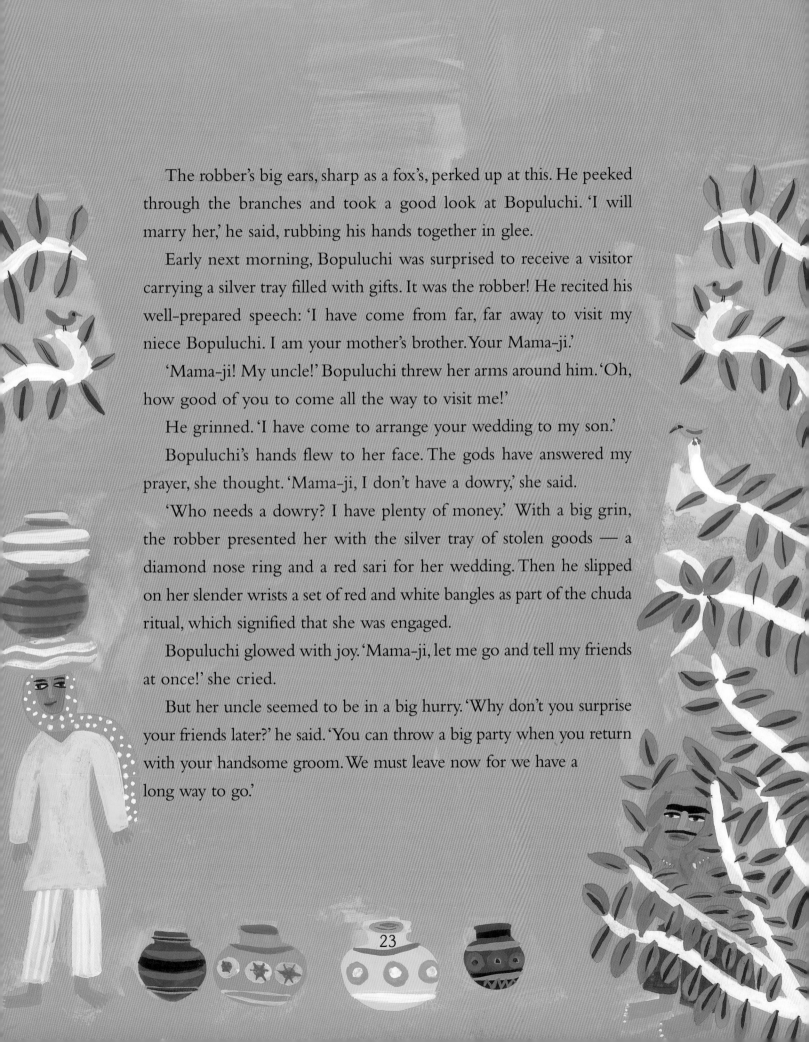

The robber's big ears, sharp as a fox's, perked up at this. He peeked through the branches and took a good look at Bopuluchi. 'I will marry her,' he said, rubbing his hands together in glee.

Early next morning, Bopuluchi was surprised to receive a visitor carrying a silver tray filled with gifts. It was the robber! He recited his well-prepared speech: 'I have come from far, far away to visit my niece Bopuluchi. I am your mother's brother. Your Mama-ji.'

'Mama-ji! My uncle!' Bopuluchi threw her arms around him. 'Oh, how good of you to come all the way to visit me!'

He grinned. 'I have come to arrange your wedding to my son.'

Bopuluchi's hands flew to her face. The gods have answered my prayer, she thought. 'Mama-ji, I don't have a dowry,' she said.

'Who needs a dowry? I have plenty of money.' With a big grin, the robber presented her with the silver tray of stolen goods — a diamond nose ring and a red sari for her wedding. Then he slipped on her slender wrists a set of red and white bangles as part of the chuda ritual, which signified that she was engaged.

Bopuluchi glowed with joy. 'Mama-ji, let me go and tell my friends at once!' she cried.

But her uncle seemed to be in a big hurry. 'Why don't you surprise your friends later?' he said. 'You can throw a big party when you return with your handsome groom. We must leave now for we have a long way to go.'

PUNJAB

So Bopuluchi packed the few things she owned, and they set off on her uncle's horse.

The monsoon season had ended and the Himalayan hills were awash with fragrant blue blossoms. What a beautiful day, thought Bopuluchi.

Soon they left the village behind. A flock of white-cheeked Himalayan bulbuls sang:

'Caw-caw-caw! Beware, beware!
Smell the danger in the air!'

Bopuluchi looked at her uncle. 'Mama-ji, Mama-ji, did you hear the birds?'

'Aah!' he said, scratching his big ears. 'They are afraid of us.'

'Oh!' said Bopuluchi, and soon she was lost in thoughts about her wedding.

The road led them to the depths of the jungle where wild hares and gerbils scurried about, and the deer roamed on the emerald green fields. Then by a creek, Bopuluchi heard some frogs croak:

'Ribbit-ribbit-ribbit! Beware, beware!
Smell the danger in the air!'

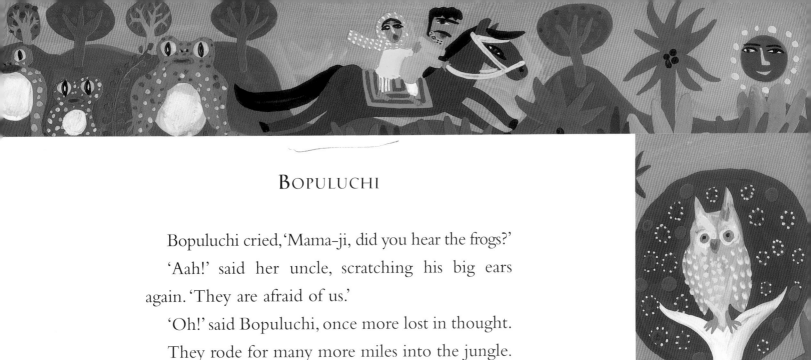

BOPULUCHI

Bopuluchi cried, 'Mama-ji, did you hear the frogs?'

'Aah!' said her uncle, scratching his big ears again. 'They are afraid of us.'

'Oh!' said Bopuluchi, once more lost in thought.

They rode for many more miles into the jungle. Soon the sun slipped behind the hills. In the dark, an owl hooted:

'Too-whit-too-too, too-whit-too-too!
Beware, beware!
Smell the danger in the air!'

Bopuluchi said, 'Mama-ji, Mama-ji, did you hear the owl?'

'Aah!' he replied. 'He's afraid of us.'

She frowned. How could the owl be afraid of them when it was up in the tree?

In a while, they reached a small, run-down house.

'Get off!' ordered Bopuluchi's uncle.

'Here?' said the startled girl.

'Hurry.' He pulled her off the horse.

Bopuluchi felt weak. Why was her uncle suddenly so rude?

'I am the Fearless Robber from Mumbai,' the man announced. 'The old woman who lives here takes care of my loot. I have no sons. I am going to marry you!'

'You liar, you cheat! I will never marry you!' Bopuluchi said fiercely.

'She will, she will. Heh! Heh!' cackled an ugly old witch, coming towards them. She found some twine which the robber then used to tie Bopuluchi to a chair. 'Don't worry. I'll take care of the pretty bird while you make the wedding arrangements.'

The robber left the house, bolting the door from the outside.

Bopuluchi began to cry when the bulbuls, frogs, and the owl sang:

'Caw-caw-caw! Ribbit-ribbit-ribbit! Too-whit-too-too!
Bopuluchi, think-think-think.
You are as witty as you are pretty.'

'Heh! Heh!' The old witch pulled Bopuluchi's long, shiny hair. 'Tell me, pretty bird, how you got such soft, fair skin and such long, shiny, black hair?'

'Go away!' cried Bopuluchi, trying to kick her.

The old witch grabbed a sharp knife out of a drawer. 'I'll chop off your hair if you don't tell, and then you'll be bald like me. Heh! Heh!'

A clever idea suddenly came to Bopuluchi. 'I'll tell you my secret,' she said.

'Tell me pretty bird, do tell me,' said the witch.

Punjab

Bopuluchi whispered, 'A magic pudding makes me nimble and spry. It makes my skin soft and silky. It makes my hair grow.'

'Make the pudding for me now,' demanded the old witch.

So far so good, Bopuluchi thought as she set out to make kheer. She boiled rice, added milk and sugar, and sprinkled cardamom, almonds and saffron to make it sweet and nutty and very tasty. Then she poured a whole bottle of liquor into it.

Bopuluchi gave the big bowl of rice pudding to the old witch. 'The more you eat, the faster your wrinkles will disappear. The faster you eat, the longer your hair will grow.'

Thick, greedy lips smacked as the old witch gulped and gobbled every bit of the pudding. Soon her eyes closed and she fell asleep, *zzzzz snort, zzzzz snuffle*. The kheer had done its work.

Quickly, Bopuluchi jumped out of the window into the darkness.

Meanwhile, the robber returned with a jug of rose sherbet and a box of sweet golden jalebi. To his surprise, he saw the old witch fast asleep at the table. He shook her awake and she told him about the magic pudding. 'Bopuluchi tricked us!' he yelled. 'By hook or by crook, I'll drag her back and marry her!'

In the meantime, Bopuluchi had reached the village and returned home. She made sure that she slept next to a bowl of flour and a long, thorny broom that night and every night after.

One night she heard a scuffling sound in her room. She knew at

BOPULUCHI

once that it was the robber. Quickly dabbing the white flour on her face, she grabbed her thorny broom and jabbed it at the figure in the dark. *Thwack! Thwaaack!*

'Help!' the robber screamed. 'Ghost!' he cried. He ran outside as fast as he could and scrambled up the tamarind tree in the garden.

'Come down, fearless robber!' yelled Bopuluchi, shaking the tree.

As the tree swayed back and forth, so did the robber. Suddenly, the branch he was holding onto snapped and he fell flat on the grass.

As quickly as he possibly could, he scrambled to his feet and hobbled away, limping on one foot, swearing never ever to return.

Years later, Bopuluchi met a fine young man who loved her for who she was, and did not care about a dowry. The whole village celebrated her wedding with feasting, music and bhangra dancing.

Bopuluchi wore a richly woven red sari. Her arms were covered with bangles and a golden tikka, or disc, crowned her forehead. Next to her was her tall and handsome groom.

Her friends gazed at him in admiration. 'He looks like a rich raja's son,' said one of them.

'A skilled archer like Arjuna,' said another friend.

'A valiant warrior as invincible as Lord Indra,' said another.

Bopuluchi lived happily ever after. But she never forgot the robber. And if you are ever invited into her house, you may still find the bowl of flour and a long, thorny broom right beside her bed.

NAGALAND

Nagaland lies in the hills and mountains of the north-eastern part of India. The people of Nagaland form sixteen major tribes, as well as many sub-tribes.

The traditional Naga religion is animistic, which means that the people regard all aspects of nature — stones, stars, plants and animals — as being alive in a spiritual way. Mala's 'friend' the peepul tree in 'Princess Mala and the Tree Spirit' belongs to this tradition.

The clothing in Nagaland is colourful and reveals not only what tribe a person belongs to, but also how wealthy and brave they are. Naga warriors traditionally carried bamboo shields, sheathed in bearskin, and wore patterned shawls. In this story, the mysterious stranger wears a warrior shawl and carries a dao — a tool with a long iron blade that has many uses, including clearing forests and cutting bamboo for building houses. Mala herself wears a sarong, a long piece of cloth wrapped round her body, and a red-gold scarf that becomes a token of love between her and her beloved peepul tree.

◆ Nagaland is a rural state. More than 85 per cent of the people live in small, isolated villages. Built on hilltops, these villages were once protected by massive wooden gates approached by narrow, sunken paths, not unlike the paths that Mala follows in this story.

◆ Each of the Naga tribes is divided into several clans, sometimes as many as twenty. The bigger the tribe, the greater the number of clans.

◆ Villages in Nagaland often have a morung, a house for young, unmarried men where trophies of war are hung. The pillars are carved with images of human and animal figures.

◆ Women hold an honourable position in Naga society. They work in the fields on an equal level with men and have great influence in the tribal councils.

◆ Weaving is a traditional art handed down through generations. Each of the tribes has its own unique designs and colours, and makes shawls, handwoven shoulder bags and table mats.

Princess Mala and the Tree Spirit

A peepul tree once stood tall and majestic in the jungle that fringed the royal gardens in the north-eastern kingdom of Nagaland. Some said the tree was blessed, that its boughs reached all the way up to heaven, while others believed it was haunted by ancestral spirits.

One day a conch shell blew long and hard from the palace to announce the birth of a baby girl to the king and queen after years of praying to the gods. Unknown to anyone, the peepul tree raised its leafy boughs to welcome Princess Mala.

Years passed, and the princess grew older. She loved to play outside. Every afternoon when the swami who tutored her gave her a break, she ran outside to the palace gardens, dancing among the fragrant flowers.

One afternoon Mala sat in the garden, her lap filled with the roses she had just picked. A butterfly alighted on her arm, flapping its wings

32

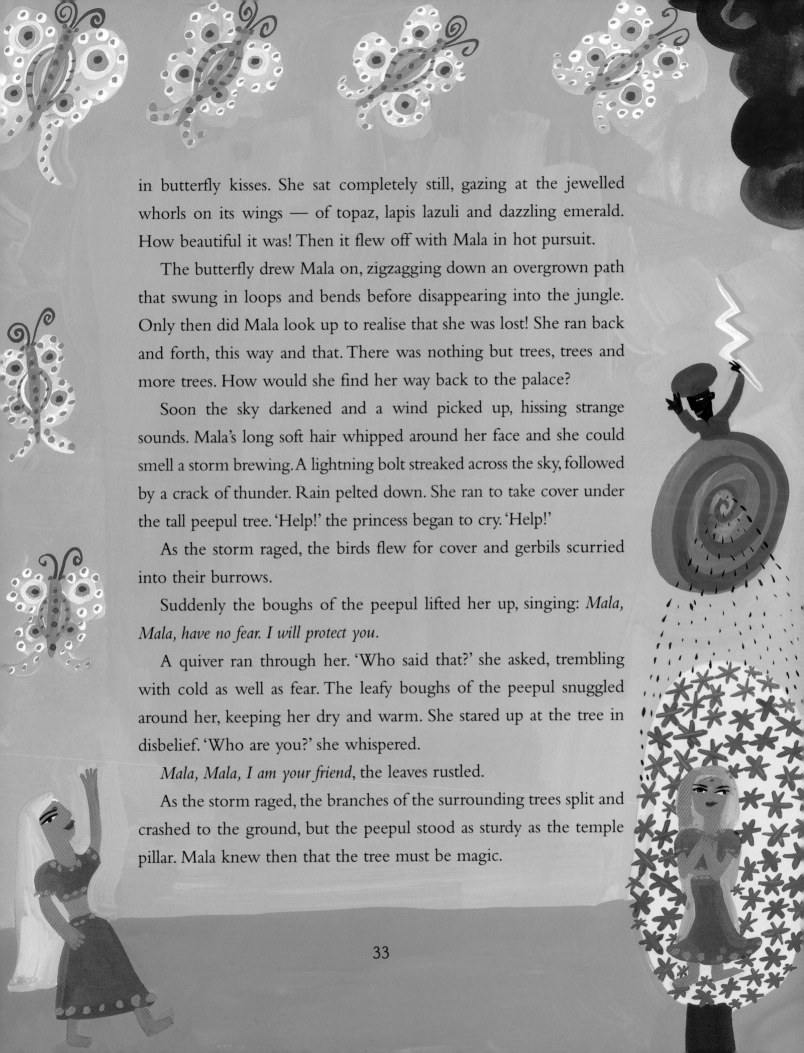

in butterfly kisses. She sat completely still, gazing at the jewelled whorls on its wings — of topaz, lapis lazuli and dazzling emerald. How beautiful it was! Then it flew off with Mala in hot pursuit.

The butterfly drew Mala on, zigzagging down an overgrown path that swung in loops and bends before disappearing into the jungle. Only then did Mala look up to realise that she was lost! She ran back and forth, this way and that. There was nothing but trees, trees and more trees. How would she find her way back to the palace?

Soon the sky darkened and a wind picked up, hissing strange sounds. Mala's long soft hair whipped around her face and she could smell a storm brewing. A lightning bolt streaked across the sky, followed by a crack of thunder. Rain pelted down. She ran to take cover under the tall peepul tree. 'Help!' the princess began to cry. 'Help!'

As the storm raged, the birds flew for cover and gerbils scurried into their burrows.

Suddenly the boughs of the peepul lifted her up, singing: *Mala, Mala, have no fear. I will protect you.*

A quiver ran through her. 'Who said that?' she asked, trembling with cold as well as fear. The leafy boughs of the peepul snuggled around her, keeping her dry and warm. She stared up at the tree in disbelief. 'Who are you?' she whispered.

Mala, Mala, I am your friend, the leaves rustled.

As the storm raged, the branches of the surrounding trees split and crashed to the ground, but the peepul stood as sturdy as the temple pillar. Mala knew then that the tree must be magic.

33

NAGALAND

When the rain stopped, Mala looked around. Everything was soaking wet, but the peepul tree was bone dry. Soon the guards came on horseback looking for Mala. They found her nestled in the branches of the peepul tree and took her home.

'Mala, you can't wander about on your own.' The king was upset.

'But a tree kept me dry in the storm,' said Mala. 'It promised to protect me.'

The king frowned. 'My dear girl, you are tired.'

But Mala knew the peepul tree was magic. From that day on, she always sneaked off to visit it.

One day, the king summoned his daughter. 'Mala,' he said. 'Soon you will be married and be the queen of another kingdom. I have invited suitors from all the neighbouring countries.'

'No!' cried Mala, horrified. 'This is my home!'

Sobbing, Mala ran through the jungle to the peepul. She buried her face in its leaves. 'Father wants me to get married,' she cried. 'What will I do?'

The peepul snuggled around her in a gentle embrace, singing: *Mala, Mala, I will always be your friend*. And she felt comforted.

PRINCESS MALA AND THE TREE SPIRIT

During the next few months, rich rajas in bejewelled robes travelled hundreds of miles to win the hand of Princess Mala.

On one particular visit, one figure stood out. She saw that his warrior shawl had the print of a tiger and in the belt around his waist was the shining dao of the Naga people. Quickly, she took her maid aside and told her what to do before she lost sight of the man.

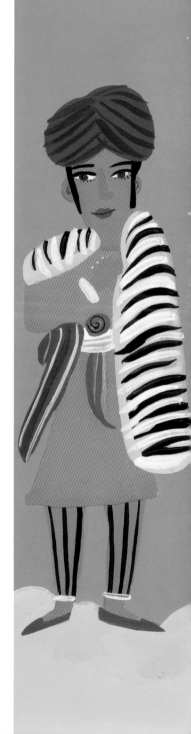

The maid sneaked up to the tall stranger and deftly tucked Mala's silken red-gold scarf into the man's dao belt. When all the suitors were leaving, the maid followed the mysterious man outside. It was dark, but she could see Mala's shiny scarf hanging from his belt. Suddenly the man disappeared into the jungle. The maid returned to give her young mistress the news. Mala was disappointed. All night, she tossed and turned and could not sleep.

Early the next day when Mala visited the peepul, she cried out in surprise. Her scarf was tied into a red knot around a branch of the tree. How did it get there? And how did the stranger know that the peepul was special to her?

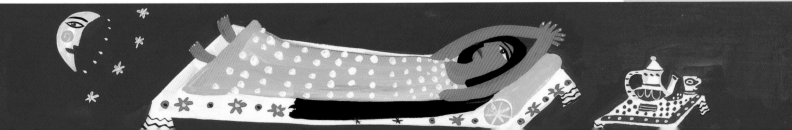

Back at the palace, the king asked, 'My dear Mala, have you selected your suitor?'

'Father . . .' she paused. 'I don't like any of them.'

The king was puzzled. The suitors were wealthy princes and came from respectable families. Surely she would be happy with one of them — or was she seeing someone else? Finally, he called his guards and asked them to keep a close watch on the princess.

The next morning when Mala went to the jungle, the guards followed her at a distance. They saw her talk to the peepul. Making a careful note of its location, they returned to the palace.

'Your Majesty, a tree spirit haunts your daughter.'

'Then cut down the tree,' commanded the king.

That evening the guards set off to fell the peepul tree, but they could not find it. They decided they would return the next morning when the sun was shining.

Meanwhile, at the palace, Mala spotted the tall dark man among her suitors once again. This time she had a clever plan that she would carry out herself. She followed the mysterious man outside. As she

NAGALAND

followed him, she broke her pearl necklace and, with every few steps, she dropped a pearl on the ground, where it shone in the light of the moon. Suddenly, the moon went behind a cloud and she was forced to return to the palace. She would have to wait till morning to see if the stranger had left any clues for her to find.

When the pale pink dawn broke over the Naga hills, Mala tiptoed out of the palace, following her trail of pearls through the gardens and into the jungle. But the trail didn't just stop, as she'd expected. To her surprise, it just kept going. More pearls had been dropped on the ground, leading on and on into the jungle. She followed the shining trail as it wound its way right up to the peepul tree!

At that very moment, there was a harsh cry. 'Make way, princess!'

The guards, armed with axes, surrounded the tree.

'No!' cried Mala. 'The peepul is my friend.'

'Sorry, we must obey the king's orders,' insisted the guards.

One guard raised his axe and struck at the tree. *Thwack!* His axe bounced off. Another guard joined in. *Thwack!* His axe bounced off as well. The last guard swung his axe with all his might against the tree. *THWACK!* Flying wood chips flew into the eyes of the guards. 'Aieeee!' cried the startled men, stepping back.

Princess Mala and the Tree Spirit

Mala threw her arms around the peepul and began to cry. As she wept, a cloud of mist arose. Tears fell on the trunk, transforming it into the torso of a man. Tears fell on the branches, turning them into arms and legs. Tears fell on the leaves, turning them into hair. Where the peepul tree had been, there stood a tall, dark, handsome man. He was the same mysterious stranger who had come to see her in the great hall at the palace and then disappeared.

Mala gasped in amazement. 'Who are you?'

The man bowed. 'I am Prince Anand. The demon Rakshasa put a curse on me. When the sun rises, I turn into a tree but when the sun sets, I become my real self. Your tears of love broke the curse.' He kissed the back of her hand and thanked her.

In a daze of happiness, Mala led the prince to meet the king and queen at the palace.

'Father!' cried Mala. 'Prince Anand is the tree spirit who protected me from the storm all those years ago.' She related the story of how the curse was now broken.

Before long, the conch shell at the palace was blowing once again, this time to announce the wedding of Princess Mala to Prince Anand. For seven days and seven nights, flutes played and drums rolled, and there was feasting and dancing throughout the kingdom of Nagaland.

UTTAR PRADESH

Uttar Pradesh is the most populated state in India, with over 166 million people. Located in the north, Uttar Pradesh covers a large part of the plains around the Ganges and Yamuna rivers.

This region was the setting for the great Sanskrit epic, the 'Mahabharata'. The classical epic is the longest poem ever composed! It describes the struggle for power between two groups of cousins from the Bharata family. Both clans wanted to rule the area between the Indus and Ganges rivers and the Himalayan mountains, which is now the state of Uttar Pradesh.

Every year tourists and pilgrims visit Allahabad and Varanasi, two of the holiest cities in India. Agra, another city, is home to the Taj Mahal, a monument that was commissioned in the seventeenth century by the Mughal Emperor Shah Jahan as a mausoleum for his wife, Mumtaz Mahal.

Uttar Pradesh is also well known for its arts and crafts, particularly saris, silks, carpets, leather crafts, metalware, cloth work and embroidery. The pottery of Uttar Pradesh is world-famous.

◆ Music is a large part of the lives of the people of Uttar Pradesh. The most popular songs are filmi, or songs from musical films.

◆ Traditional music and dance are performed in temples, at festivals, and at ceremonial gatherings at home. Street magic shows and episodes from religious texts are dramatically staged in urban and rural areas.

◆ Indian literature has a long history. The earliest literary traditions of India were mostly oral and were later transcribed, which was the case with the 'Mahabharata'.

◆ Interwoven with the tales of the feud of the 'Mahabharata' is the love story of Damayanti and Nala. During weddings in modern day India, it is traditional for songs praising Damayanti's love for Nala to be sung, reminding the bridal couple of their loyalty and devotion.

◆ The architecture of Uttar Pradesh has had many influences, from religious to cultural to regional. Some of the earliest examples were Buddhist — this tradition included stupas (burial mounds of earth and stone) built in the third century BC.

◆ The Taj Mahal took more than a decade to complete. It is made of pure white marble inlaid with gold, silver and thousands of gemstones.

Damayanti and Nala

Long ago, on the night when the moon and Venus crossed paths over the kingdom of Vidharbha, the celestial stars stood still, and the most beautiful maiden was born. She was named Princess Damayanti. As she grew up, people said, 'Damayanti is as lovely as a heavenly nymph.'

At the very same time in the neighbouring kingdom of Nishadha, the most handsome prince in the world was born. He was called Prince Nala. As he grew up, people said, 'Nala will be the foremost of the rajas.' Astrologers said, 'Nala will bring fame and fortune.'

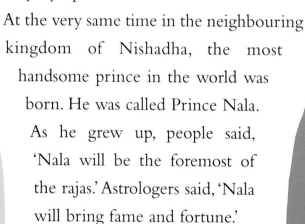

42

Years passed and the fame of the young princess's beauty spread like the scent of the champa flower. One day when Nala was on a hunting trip with his companions in Vidharbha, he caught a glimpse of Damayanti and was spellbound. From that moment on, all of his thoughts were of her. How would he let her know of his love?

Soon afterwards, Nala was feeding the swans at his father's palace garden, when he saw a pink lotus. He plucked it and took it to the oldest of the swans. 'Please take this lotus to Princess Damayanti as a token of my love for her.'

'I will, o prince,' said the old swan, taking the lotus in his beak.

'We will all go, we will all go,' cried the other swans. They flapped their wings and flew through the wide, blue sky towards the kingdom of Vidharbha.

That afternoon as Damayanti sat in the garden, she saw a mass of birds descend on the pond with a flurry of white feathers. The swans began to sing:

'Damayanti, hear! If you are the pearl of women, Nala is the pride of men. Damayanti, hear! Nala is your true love just as you are his.'

The oldest swan drew near Damayanti and dropped the pink lotus on her lap. 'Please accept this gift as a token of love from Prince Nala of Nishadha.'

Damayanti blushed. Since her fourteenth birthday she had been sent portraits of local rajas who were seeking her hand in marriage. Of all the portraits she had seen, she liked Nala's the most. She stroked the swan, thanking him and said, 'I will return the lotus to Nala at my swayamvara next week.'

Damayanti's heart sang as she stepped inside the palace. 'Father, I am ready to choose a husband.'

The king and queen embraced their only daughter with delight. A message was sent to all the neighbouring kingdoms announcing Damayanti's swayamvara. The palace was made ready. Red, green, blue and saffron brocades were draped over divans, tables adorned with fragrant flowers and sumptuous food, and Kashmiri carpets strewn across the cool, marble floors.

Soon the kingdom of Vidharbha resounded with the booming of drums and fanfares of trumpets as painted elephants in colourful garlands carried hopeful rajas into the city. Nala arrived in a gilded chariot pulled by finely decorated stallions.

DAMAYANTI AND NALA

Damayanti's beauty had stirred even the gods. Up in the heavens, four of them wanted to marry her. They were Agni, Lord of Fire; Indra, Lord of Storms; Varuna, Lord of Seas; and Yama, Lord of Death. They knew she liked Nala, but they were hopeful. 'She will choose one of us over Nala — after all he's just a mortal,' they told each other. Then, they made a plan and leapt into their heavenly chariots and descended to earth to woo the princess.

On the day of the swayamvara, Damayanti's parents sat on their thrones in the great hall, their handmaidens fanning them with peacock feathers. The suitors filed through the gilded portal to present themselves. Among them was Nala.

The drums sounded. Then everyone fell silent as Damayanti glided into the room in a flowing white sari that billowed around her willowy figure. Her long black hair was threaded with jasmine blossoms and her slender hands carried the pink lotus. Everyone gazed at her in admiration.

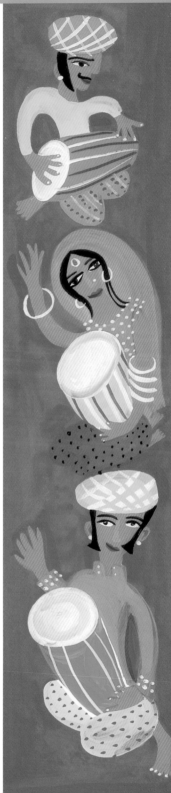

Uttar Pradesh

Damayanti took her seat beside her parents, her nutmeg eyes cast down. Her gaze rose slightly as the names of all her suitors were announced. The four gods had also come, but she searched for one face only. Nala! There he was. She looked into his gentle, trusting eyes and his face lit up. The swans' song played in her head and her heart was filled with tenderness.

But as she rose to give the lotus, she was overcome with confusion. There were five identical Nalas seated next to each other! Fear clutched her. Which one of them was the real Nala? The gods must have tricked her. Determined not to be fooled, she asked, 'Who among you is Nala?'

'I am,' said the five voices together.

Damayanti looked at the five identical men. Four of them stared with unblinking eyes. Only one man's eyes flickered. She knew that gods do not blink. She studied their faces. Four of them were unblemished. Only one was creased and shiny with sweat. She knew that gods do not sweat.

Damayanti looked down, thinking carefully. Across the floor, only one shadow fell on the marble floor. She knew that gods do not cast shadows. Her heart filled with hope.

She looked for one last proof. The marigolds in the garlands around the necks of four men were fresh and crisp. Only one man's marigolds looked half wilted. He was the man who blinked, sweated and cast a shadow. He was Nala!

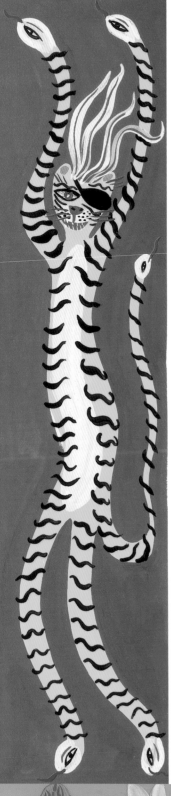

UTTAR PRADESH

'I choose you,' said Damayanti, and she held his gaze as she gave him the lotus.

Drums and sitars played and there was great rejoicing. The guests sang and drank and danced. The four gods conceded their loss, gave Damayanti and Nala their blessings and departed. On their way back to heaven, they ran into the evil demon, Rakshasa. He appeared as a roguish old tiger, one eye covered by a leather patch, frazzled white hair spiked and bristling. 'I am off to make Damayanti my bride,' he bragged.

'You cannot,' said the gods. 'She has already chosen Prince Nala.'

'Arrrg!' cried Rakshasa. Fire shot out of his mouth. 'I curse Nala.' His red, bloodshot eye glinted with malice. 'I will get Damayanti!'

'Stay away!' warned the gods.

'Heeeeheee!' Rakshasa laughed his demon laugh and danced his demon dance with his snaky arms:

'I am as evil as evil can be. I will get Damayanti, you will see.'

He took one flying leap and landed on earth. He changed into his human form and secretly watched the newly-wed couple. Nala was devout. Every morning he asked the gods for their blessings and

DAMAYANTI AND NALA

protection. Rakshasa grew impatient. Then, he learned two things that would help him. First, he discovered that Nala's brother was jealous of Nala. Second, he found out that Nala loved to play dice.

One morning, Nala forgot to ask the gods for their blessings. Rakshasa's moment had arrived. First he entered the mind of Nala's brother. 'Play!' he urged. 'I will enter the dice and help you win.'

The two brothers played all day and all night. Slowly, Nala gambled away his entire kingdom. He returned to Damayanti, humiliated. 'If you wish to leave me, I understand,' he told her. Damayanti stood firm. 'I will come with you wherever you go.'

And so it came about that Nala and Damayanti gave up their kingdom. For many months they lived in the jungle, surviving on fruit and roots and fish from the river. Damayanti grew pale and weary, but her love for Nala never wavered.

'Arrrg!' Rakshasa gnashed his sharp teeth. Soon, though, he had thought of another plan. He slipped into Nala's mind and tormented him every day. 'You're a failure, a total failure! You have destroyed Damayanti's happiness. Leave her, leave her, leave her. She's better off without you.'

UTTAR PRADESH

A bitter battle waged within Nala. The stronger Rakshasa grew, the weaker Nala became. Finally, poisoned by Rakshasa, Nala decided to follow the voice in his head. He would leave Damayanti.

And so one moonless night, Nala stole away. Damayanti awoke to find her husband gone. 'Nala! Nala!' she called out in despair.

For many days and nights she searched frantically for Nala. Thorny branches slapped her in the face, tore her sari and scratched her skin, but she went on until she was exhausted. Tearfully, she made her way to her father's palace. The four gods protected her and guided her on her journey.

One night, Damayanti saw an asoka tree and a flicker of hope lit up in her heart. The asoka symbolised life with no sadness. She walked round and round the tree, pleading, 'O asoka, please end my sorrows!' On her third round, the leaves of the tree shook and a scarlet blossom fell to her feet. Now, she knew that Nala would return to her. She picked up the flower, inhaled its heady scent, and put it in her hair.

Meanwhile, Nala drifted aimlessly in the jungle, too miserable to tell night from day. The four gods decided they must act, so they sent the Serpent King, Karkotaka, down to meet him. The serpent sprang on Nala, wrapping him in its coils and hissing, 'I have been sent to remove Rakshasa's curse.' Then Karkotaka bit Nala in the arm, and disappeared. Nala passed out.

When he came around, he began to vomit, and the venom of Rakshasa's curse left his body. Slowly, his memory returned, and he

DAMAYANTI AND NALA

was overcome with grief. How could he have left Damayanti? She was his life. He would win her back.

Nala ran towards the kingdom of King Bhima. The sky turned dark and rain fell in torrents. Chilled to the bone, he kept on running, whispering *Damayanti* at every step, his eyes blazing. When he entered Vidharbha, everyone looked at him with suspicion. At last, he stumbled up to the palace gate and begged one of the guards to call the princess.

Damayanti was startled to see a man in dishevelled rags. Drawing closer, she saw beyond the unkempt brown curls and her heart filled with tenderness. He was Nala! He knelt, begging for her forgiveness. Without hesitating, Damayanti embraced him. After all of their trials, the couple were together once more. Rakshasa had been defeated.

But Nala still had a score to settle. With Damayanti's consent, he challenged his brother to a final game of dice. On the day of the game, Damayanti fasted and prayed for justice. The gods conferred their blessings on him. With a single throw, Nala won the game. His kingdom was restored, and he and Damayanti lived happily as King and Queen of Nishadha.

Today, it is said the loving couple lie entwined in a grave where an asoka tree with fragrant red blossoms has grown. Those who visit the site circle the tree three times and gather its blossoms, hoping to attain the true love of Damayanti and Nala.

TAMIL NADU

Tamil Nadu is the southernmost state of India. Its Hindu temples are famous — there are more than 30,000! It would take years to see them all.

Tamil Nadu is the home of ancient Dravidian art and culture. The elaborate Dravidian temples have wonderful towers called gopuras, which were built very high, and according to tradition are meant to touch the heavens. They are often decorated with mythical animals and monsters, meant to protect the gods.

In 'Priya's Magic Bowl' Priya knows that she too can find protection in the temple, away from her vicious stepmother, and with the help of the kindly swami, a religious teacher who lives at the temple. She goes to pray to Durga, the Hindu mother-goddess, who watches over Priya, bringing her good fortune in the form of the magic bowl. Among the delicious foods that it brings forth are pilaf, a spiced rice dish; and gulab jamun, milk balls in a sweet syrup flavoured with cardamom.

- Tamil is an ancient language and its literature includes two great epics, the *Silappadikaram* — the 'Tale of the Anklet' — and the *Manimekhalai* — the story of a temple dancer with a magic bowl like Priya's.

- Most of the arts and crafts traditions of Tamil Nadu can be traced back to the influence of the temples. Working in the temples helped refine the craftsmen's skills, which they applied to other items that they made.

- Historically, the temples were mainly a place of worship, but they were also a place for social gatherings, education and celebrations.

- Rice is the staple food of Tamil Nadu. Favourite rice dishes include idli or rice patties; dosa or rice pancakes; and vadai or lentil doughnuts.

- The amazing Nataraja Temple, built in the ninth century, is dedicated to the god Shiva as the Cosmic Lord of Dance. It features a gopura with sculptures of the 108 hand and feet movements of Bharat Natyam, a classic temple dance.

- Many towns in Tamil Nadu start with the word Tiru, meaning 'sacred', indicating the location of a major religious site.

Priya's Magic Bowl

There once was a little girl called Priya who lived with her loving father and her stepmother in Tamil Nadu in southern India. Priya's stepmother was attractive and well dressed, but if you looked at her closely you could see a steely glint in her eyes. Priya was as radiant as a lotus flower, but her soft, doe-like eyes looked dark and sad. Her mother had died a few years ago and her father, being a pedlar, was always on the road. Poor Priya was stuck at home, attending to her cruel stepmother's every whim.

When Priya's father was at home with them, her stepmother would call for Priya in a voice as sweet and rich as honey. 'Pretty Priya, where are you?' she'd sing. However, when he was away on business, her sharp tongue sliced through the air like a butcher's knife. 'Silly girl, come here at once!' she'd shout, and 'Slow slug, you're taking too long!' Whatever Priya did, it was never good enough.

On the morning of her twelfth birthday, Priya woke up feeling especially sad. Her father had left on a long trip the week before and not returned. She bowed before the idol of Goddess Durga that her mother had given her. 'Durga Ma, help me,' she prayed. Before she had finished, she heard her stepmother yell for her and she sprang to her feet.

Her stepmother stood waiting with that evil glint in her eye and a wide shark-grin on her face. 'Now you're old enough to earn your own living,' she said. She scraped last night's rice from the pot, wrapped it in a dirty cloth and thrust the bundle into Priya's frail hands. 'Go!' And she shoved Priya out of the house, slamming the door behind her.

Priya stared at the big, blue sky above, sobbing bitterly. Where would she go? With whom would she live? Her aunts and uncles lived hundreds of miles away and the few friends she had were poor. How could she thrust upon them the burden of yet another mouth to feed?

She walked and walked until her legs ached and she became so tired, she could walk no longer. She stopped in a park by a big banyan tree. Nobody will chase me away from here, she thought. She tied her bundle of food onto a branch of the banyan and sat down to rest among the twisting roots of the tree. Within minutes, she was asleep.

As she slept, the plump green fruit of the banyan tree burst open, and out jumped several tiny forest nymphs, the vanadevata. They saw

Tamil Nadu

Priya sleeping below and a bundle hanging on the branch above. They untied the bundle and tasted the stale rice inside. 'Crunchy,' they said. The vanadevata had never eaten stale rice before; they always ate soft, sweet dishes in the heaven where they lived. They looked at Priya lying fast asleep and liked her kind eyes. 'Before we leave, we will give the little girl something in return,' they decided.

When Priya woke up, she was hungry. She brought down her bundle from the branch of the banyan and untied it. The rice was gone and in its place was an empty clay bowl. She held the bowl in her hands, and her eyes filled with tears. 'Who ate my food?' she cried.

At once, the tiny vanadevata rose out of the bowl. Bowing before Priya, they said, 'We are spirits of the forest and we're very sorry we ate your rice. To make up for it, we will bring you any food you want. What would you like to eat?'

Priya blinked, dumbstruck. The only person who had ever asked her what she wanted to eat had been her mother, and that had been so long ago, she had almost forgotten it.

PRIYA'S MAGIC BOWL

'What would you like to eat?' the vanadevata asked her again.

Priya was starving. 'Anything at all,' she said.

The vanadevata served Priya with plates of spicy curries, saffron rice, ripe red pomegranates, and pawpaw as sweet as honey.

'Thank you,' cried Priya, her heart full of gratitude. 'Thank you so much!' She folded her hands together as if in prayer, thanking the spirits, knowing that Durga Ma must have sent them. She started to eat the delicious food but found she could not finish it. 'This is too much,' she said.

The vanadevata duly appeared. They took away the leftovers and dirty dishes. 'The clay bowl we left will always provide for you if you hold it in your hands and call for us,' they said. Then they bowed before Priya and disappeared.

Priya clutched the clay bowl. It was magic! She would never go hungry again. She ran home as fast as she could to tell her stepmother.

But her stepmother would not let Priya inside. 'Stop making up stories, girl! Go away! Just go!' And she pushed Priya out.

As Priya walked, she remembered how her mother had told her the story of Durga Ma and how the goddess would always protect her, so she set off with her bowl to the temple. There she met a swami, who kindly let her stay at the temple. The magic bowl provided all her meals, as the vanadevata had told her it would. But after a few days, she thought to herself: *'What use is so much food if I can't share it with others?'*

So, accompanied by the swami, she went from door to door in the neighbourhood and invited the people for a meal at the temple. She also went home to invite her parents.

When her stepmother saw Priya, her eyes became slits and she gave a big sniff. 'Silly girl! Why did you come back? Your father isn't here, you know.'

'I have come to invite Father and you to a meal at the temple tomorrow evening,' said Priya, not in the least deterred.

'Huh!' The stepmother sneered. 'To eat a meal of berries and bones, I've no doubt. Huh!' She laughed. She laughed so hard that she clutched her stomach and nearly fell over. She had no intention of going to the temple to eat with Priya, nor would she tell her husband about the invitation.

In the evening, a big crowd of poor townspeople gathered for the meal. They sat on the grass in the temple garden as Priya brought out her clay bowl.

'What a fine bowl!' they said.

TAMIL NADU

Priya told them how she got it and how Durga Ma had blessed her. She clutched the bowl and said, 'Heavenly forest spirits, please feed my guests with your gracious gifts.' The bewildered townspeople held their breaths and waited.

Lo and behold! Tiny vanadevata rose out of the bowl, carrying silver platters filled with spicy curries, saffron pilaf, almond kheer and gulab jamu.

As the guests ate, new dishes arrived, and the lovely nymphs served them readily. The people ate and ate. They ate so much that they had trouble getting up and carrying themselves home.

Soon the whole town was buzzing with the story of Priya's miraculous bowl and the sumptuous food it had given the guests to eat. People chatted about the heavenly forest spirits and how the gods had smiled upon the little girl. When Priya's stepmother heard the news, she bit her lips till they bled. How could her stepdaughter have done so well for herself, she thought. Then her bruised lips curled into a greedy smile. 'I will do the same thing as Priya,' she said.

PRIYA'S MAGIC BOWL

So, next morning Priya's stepmother packed some golden laddus, fried sweets, in a clean cloth and walked to the park. She sat under the same banyan tree where Priya had sat. She closed her eyes, pretending to be asleep. She was scheming that when the forest creatures appeared, she would ask them to bring her jewellery, silk saris and gold coins. As she waited and waited, she grew sleepy. Soon she was snoring.

The vanadevata heard the loud snoring and came out. They saw the bundle of food on the branch of the tree and thought it must belong to Priya. They untied the bundle and tasted the golden laddus inside. 'Ughhhh!' they cried and spat the sweets out. The food tasted of evil intentions. Then they saw Priya's stepmother slumped fast asleep beneath the tree. 'Ughhhh!' they cried again. 'She looks like a wicked witch!' They left an odd-shaped wooden bowl in the bundle and disappeared.

When Priya's stepmother woke up, she bit her bruised lip, upset that she had fallen asleep. She

knew she'd probably missed the vanadevata and the opportunity to ask them for jewellery, saris and gold coins. Quickly, she rose and grabbed her bundle from the branch. She saw the half-eaten golden laddus inside and shoved them into her mouth. 'Too bad they didn't finish them.' Then she saw the wooden bowl and laughed. 'That was so easy, so easy!'

Priya's stepmother hurried home with the bowl and invited all her rich friends to a grand banquet. Thankfully, she did not have to invite Priya as her father was still away.

In the evening, Priya's stepmother stood resplendent in gold jewellery and a sari of Madras silk, looking as pleased as a peacock as she welcomed the rich guests to her house.

The guests sat on soft, cushioned chairs. Priya's stepmother brought out her wooden bowl and placed it on the big table for everyone to see. 'Now for the magic,' she said. She ordered a long list of exotic foods.

The guests leaned forward eagerly, their gaze fixed on the bowl. There was a long silence. No one came to serve them. The guests waited and waited. They had fasted all day, hoping the meal would be as good as Priya's was reported to have been. They sighed and shrugged and shuffled in their increasing discomfort.

Priya's stepmother banged the wooden bowl repeatedly against the table. 'Hurry up, lazy creatures! We are hungry.'

Lo and behold! Dozens of snakes slithered out of the bowl, their

forked tongues flickering, and began to hiss. Priya's stepmother shrieked, and the terrified guests ran away. And as they ran, the snakes darted outside, disappearing into the long grass. As for Priya's stepmother, she felt so embarrassed that her head drooped with shame and remorse. How would she look anyone in the face again?

When Priya's father returned from his travels, his wife explained why his daughter wasn't there to greet him. 'Priya did not want to work and so she ran away. She has shamed us. We must leave the town at once.'

The pedlar was puzzled. He did not believe his wife. He knew Priya would never leave him. 'I cannot live without my ladkhi, my dear Priya. I will look for her and bring her back.'

After earnestly searching for three days and nights, he found Priya at the temple. She was praying to Goddess Durga Ma.

'My ladkhi! My girl!' He held Priya close and hugged her tearfully. 'Why did you go away?'

Priya told him everything.

'Please come home,' he begged. 'Your stepmother will not live with us any more.'

Priya agreed. She said goodbye to the swami, took her bowl and left with her father. On reaching home, they found that her stepmother had already gone. And so Priya lived happily with her father. Her magic bowl always provided them with the very best food, and she always shared it with others.

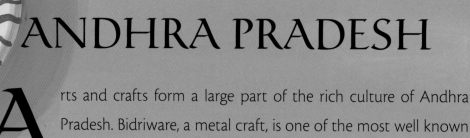

ANDHRA PRADESH

Arts and crafts form a large part of the rich culture of Andhra Pradesh. Bidriware, a metal craft, is one of the most well known of its handicrafts. It is the art of making intricate patterns of silver on matt black metal. Other arts in Andhra Pradesh include weaving, music, lacquerware, pearl jewellery and painting. Techniques and skills were often passed down through the generations by gurus.

A guru can be a teacher of a craft or a spiritual guide, like Guruji in 'Five Men in a Cart'. The role of gurus is important in Hinduism, Sikhism and Buddhism. Gurus give up all material possessions, including their homes, occupations and families, in order to teach others — their students are likely to be rather brighter than the four disciples in this story! Spiritual teachers meditate in isolated places in the forest or mountains in simple shacks called 'ashrams'. In ancient India these ashrams were like community schools. Over time, the ashrams became gurukuls, a larger type of school that eventually evolved into the modern-day university.

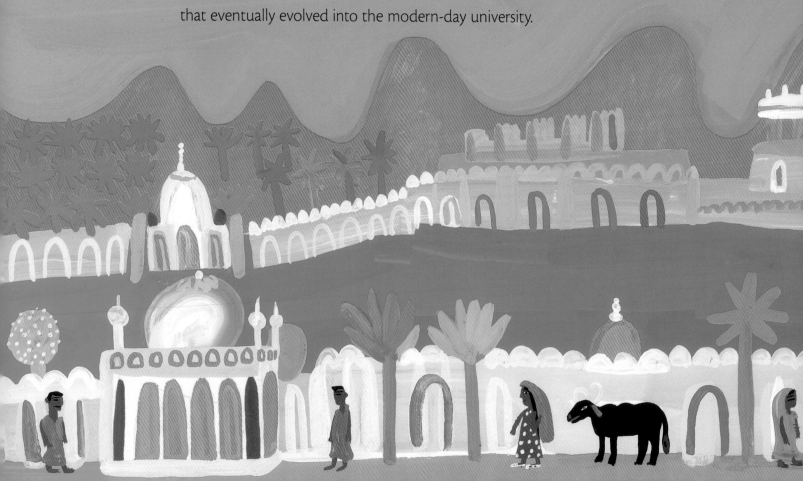

- ◆ Experienced gurus taught more than sixty subjects, including languages, grammar, philosophy, music, dance, medicine, surgery, politics and law.

- ◆ The kuchipudi dance comes from Andhra Pradesh. Famous for its grace and charm, it is very dramatic and performers act out scenes from the great epics.

- ◆ Handwoven saris are made all over Andhra Pradesh. Vibrant and unique, the saris are named after the city where they are made.

- ◆ In this story, Guruji's disciples are dressed simply in dhotis, or loincloths, and kurtas, long, collarless shirts.

- ◆ Tholubommalata or puppetry is an ancient tradition. Performers use every type of puppet, whether operated by strings or rods or glove; or shadow puppets, to tell mythological tales.

- ◆ Bonalu, known as the 'Dance of the Balancing Pots', is a celebration where brightly-dressed female dancers balance pots while stepping to rhythmic beats and tunes in praise of the village god.

Five Men in a Cart

ive men from the ashram set off in a bullock cart to sell produce from their garden and to buy provisions at the local market. They were Guruji the teacher, in a bright saffron turban, and his four very enthusiastic, very obedient disciples, all in white dhotis and kurtas.

Guruji urged his men, 'Your guru is like a cow, ever ready to give milk for your benefit. So always, always, follow your guru's orders.'

'Ji ha,' said the four men together, their heads wobbling in agreement.

Guruji went on. 'Make sure you take the essentials to eat and drink. We will not stop at all as I want to reach the market by noon.'

'Ji ha,' said the four men. They loaded the cart

with a big black pot of rice, jars of water, and a basket filled with fruit and vegetables for selling at the market. They sat in the soft, hay-lined wagon at the back. The cart was drawn by two bullocks with tinkling brass bells on their thick necks, tolling *doh, doh, dong* as the wheels of the cart rattled *thup, thup, thup* along the rugged road.

It was a beautiful day and the morning breeze tickled their noses. Soon Guruji dozed off, and his head rolled from side to side. On the way, the cart swerved to avoid a troop of monkeys. It gave a big jolt and Guruji's turban slipped off his head and fell on to the road.

'Stop!' cried two of the men. 'We must pick up Guruji's turban.' 'No!' cried the other two men. 'Don't you remember? Guruji doesn't want to stop at all. He wants to reach the market by noon.'

The men did not know what to do. They looked at Guruji for guidance, but their teacher's chest rose and fell with rattling snores.

They continued the journey and the bullock cart wound its way along the road that skirted the edge of the river. High above, the sun blazed fiercely. Guruji woke up, feeling very hot. He stroked his bald, damp head. 'Where is my turban?' he shouted.

Guruji seemed very angry. The four men looked at each other. Then one of them said, 'Guruji, it fell when the cart jolted!'

'Then why didn't you pick it up?'

ANDHRA PRADESH

The four men shrugged uneasily. 'Guruji, you told us not to stop at all,' they said together.

'Silly, silly men!' Guruji slapped at his forehead in frustration. 'How will I go to the market without my turban? Turn back at once. I need my turban!'

'Ji ha,' said the four men together, and they all wobbled their heads in agreement.

The cart turned back towards the ashram. Soon the men spotted the bright saffron turban on the road. They stopped the cart, picked up the turban and gave it to their teacher.

Guruji placed it on his head and wagged his finger at the four men. 'Next time, pick up ANYTHING that falls on the road! Do you understand me? Do you?'

'Ji ha,' said the four men, wobbling their heads.

'Now hurry up or we will never reach the market in time.'

'Ji ha,' said the four men, wobbling their heads once again.

The five men in the bullock cart set off for the market once more. Further along the road, Guruji dozed off again.

Soon the droppings of the bullocks fell heavily onto the road. *Plop! Plop! Plop!*

FIVE MEN IN A CART

The four men looked at each other, horrified. They were supposed to pick up anything that fell on the road.

'Stop!' cried two men. 'We must pick up the dung, even if it is filthy. We must obey Guruji.'

'No!' said the other two. 'We will be late for the market!'

The four men argued for a while. They looked at their sleeping teacher and recalled his orders — to pick up ANYTHING that fell on the road.

Finally, they stopped the cart and the four men leapt out. They scooped the dung off the road and dropped it into the back of the cart, even though it made their hands filthy, even though they felt squeamish doing it.

The cart rumbled on. Guruji woke and saw the pile of brown dung in the wagon next to him and asked, 'What is this?'

'Bullock dung,' explained the four men. 'It fell on the road so we picked it up.'

Guruji turned as red as cherry. 'Silly, silly men! Stop! Get this dung off at once and clean the cart and your hands.'

'Ji ha,' said the four men. The cart stopped. The men scooped the dung out the wagon then went to the river to wash their hands.

When they returned, Guruji had calmed down. 'I have made a list of all the essentials to be picked up if they fall off the cart.' He handed the list to them. 'Now, for your guru's sake, please follow this list. DO NOT pick up anything that is not on the list. Is that clear?'

'Ji ha,' said the four men, wobbling their heads in agreement. They read out the list:

Guruji's turban
The basket of fruit and vegetables
The pot of boiled rice
Jars of water

The five men in the bullock cart set off for the market once more. On their way, the cart ran into a tree and rolled over. Guruji fell into a deep, muddy ditch, while two of the men were flung on one side of the ditch and the other two were flung on the other side, along with the basket, the fruit, vegetables, pot of rice, and the jars of water.

The men went through their teacher's checklist to see what had fallen out of the cart: 'Guruji's turban did not fall. The basket of fruit and vegetables fell.' They picked up the basket, but left the fruit and vegetables scattered on the road. 'The pot of boiled rice fell.' They picked up the pot, but left the rice. 'The jars of water fell.' They picked them up.

'Help!' cried Guruji. 'Get me out of here.'

ANDHRA PRADESH

The four men shook their heads in unison. 'Guruji, you are not on the checklist you gave us.'

'Help! Help!' cried Guruji, struggling to get out of the ditch, but falling face down into the sticky mire. His white gown and face were soiled brown.

The four men looked at each other in confusion. 'He is testing us,' said one of them. 'This is a hard test, but we must follow his list.'

'Help! Help! Help!' cried Guruji again.

The four men looked helplessly at their teacher. 'We can jump into the ditch with you if you want.'

An old woman collecting twigs for firewood heard Guruji's cries and ran to help. She held out a long twig to him. 'Hold on to this,' she said and pulled and pulled. Guruji clung on to the other end of the twig, but slipped and sank back into the sticky mire. The old

FIVE MEN IN A CART

woman suddenly caught sight of the four men standing still like temple pillars. 'Stop gawking!' she cried. 'Come and help me.'

The four men shook their heads sadly. 'We must follow Guruji's checklist and he is not on it.'

'Give me that list.' The old woman grabbed it from the men and threw it to Guruji, who hastily scrawled his name on it. Then, and only then, did the four men pull their teacher out of the ditch and help him back on to the bullock cart!

'Turn back. We are not going to the market,' said the upset Guruji.

'Ji ha,' said the four very obedient but very bewildered men.

And so for the very last time, the bullock cart with the five men ploughed back along the rugged road, *thup*, *thup*, *thup*, while the brass bells on the necks of the bullocks tolled *doh*, *doh*, *dong* all the way back to the ashram.

RAJASTHAN

Rajasthan, in north-western India, is known as 'The Land of the Kings.' Rajasthani women dress in vivid colours — deep red, stunning yellow, lively green, brilliant orange — and highlight them with sparkling gold and silver jewellery. The Rajasthani men dress in plain robes, but wear vibrant turbans.

Dance and music are very popular in Rajasthan, and there are many fairs and festivals. 'Shaira's Secret' is set at the time of Divaali, the 'Festival of Lights' that marks the Hindu New Year. A rangoli design, made from coloured sand or rice powder, is drawn on every doorstep to welcome guests. At night on the day of Lakshmi Puja, every home is filled with divas, or little clay lamps, to attract Lakshmi, the goddess of fortune, so that she will bless the household. The divas symbolise the triumph of the 'light' (truth) over the 'darkness' (evil), and in the story it is the 'light of honesty' in Shaira's heart that brings special blessings upon her family.

◆ Not only do the people of Rajasthan dress colourfully, but also their architecture is brightly coloured — the capital, Jaipur, is known as the 'Pink City' because the buildings on the main street are pink.

◆ Rajasthan was once made up of twenty-two different states, each ruled by a separate prince, or maharaja.

◆ In the city of Jodhpur there is a huge fort known as the Mehrangarh. It was built on top of a giant rock and seems to rise straight out of the hill.

◆ Rajasthan has two famous national parks. Keoladeo Ghana is one of the world's most important bird sanctuaries, and Ranthambore is a renowned game sanctuary and tiger reserve.

◆ In ancient times, Rajasthan was part of the Mauryan Empire (321–185 BC), which was the first great civilisation in India.

◆ The most popular folk dance of Rajasthan is the ghoomar, a dance traditionally performed by the royal women of Jaipur.

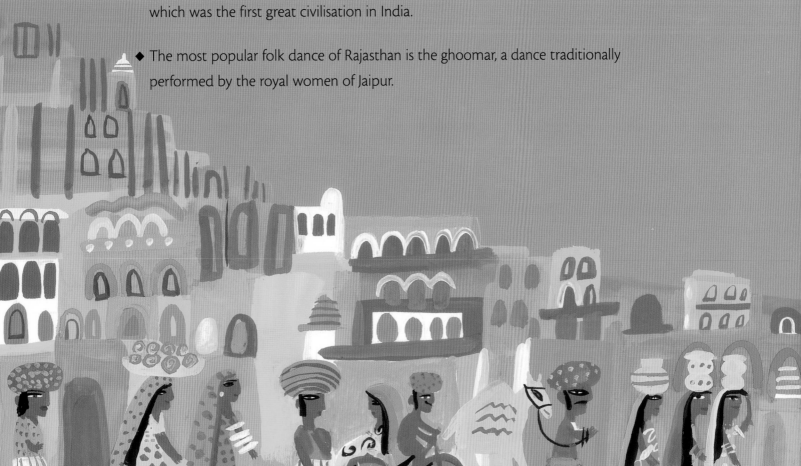

Shaira's Secret

Long ago, when gods and goddesses visited people's homes, a young girl named Shaira lived with her widowed mother in the slums by the river. Every day, Shaira went from home to home along the narrow alleys to collect dirty laundry, which her mother washed. Every day she prayed to Lakshmi, the goddess of fortune, for blessings so Ma would not have to be a washerwoman for ever.

One morning, Shaira dawdled on her way home, thinking soon it would be Divaali, the Festival of Lights. What gift would she give Ma? The shrieking crows overhead broke into her thoughts. Clamped into the beak of the leading crow was something shiny. Other crows flew after it, trying to snatch the tempting prize.

76

Cawwwww! the lead crow shrieked, and the shiny object in its beak dropped to the ground. Shaira ran as fast as her small legs could carry her to see the object. Right on the doorstep of her home, where she had drawn the rangoli design of a lotus flower by a pot of marigolds, there was a seven-string pearl necklace!

Shaira's trembling fingers felt the smooth, round beads of the necklace. She gazed longingly at it. In the sun, the colour of the lustrous beads along each of the strands changed from white to yellow, orange, red, green, blue, indigo and violet — all the colours of the rainbow! Her heartbeat quickened. The necklace would be a wonderful Divaali gift for Ma. Her mother did not own any jewellery.

Shaira ran inside, wrapped the necklace in her jasmine-scented handkerchief, and hid the small package under her mattress.

The next day was the first day of Divaali. Shaira woke early to help her mother with the laundry. Ma had promised to buy her firecrackers that exploded into a fountain of colours. Most of all, she wanted to give Ma the secret gift.

By the time Shaira finished collecting the laundry, the sun shone high in the sky. As she headed for the river bank where her mother waited, the thunder of drumbeats sounded in a nearby alley. Everybody ran to see what the commotion was. Shaira rushed with the crowd, the bundle of laundry clasped in her hands.

RAJASTHAN

The city square teemed with people. 'Hear ye all, hear ye all,' cried the king's heralds. 'Her Majesty, the queen, has lost her pearl necklace. The king will grant a big reward to anyone who finds it.'

Shaira felt her very life sucked out of her. Could it . . . could it be the necklace she had found? She turned to the lady next to her and asked, 'How did the queen lose her necklace?'

'Don't you know?' replied the lady. 'A crow snatched it from the river shore while she bathed.'

A crow? Shaira's shoulders sagged. The necklace she had found had been dropped by a crow.

The lady continued. 'It's very special. The pearls in it are extremely rare. Do you know, a thousand divers dived deep into the ocean to gather them?'

Shaira's grip on the bundle of laundry tightened. She went to find her mother, walking very slowly, carefully measuring each footstep, wondering what to do. The necklace she found must belong to the queen.

Shaira's mother, squatting at the river bank, took the bundle of clothes from her daughter.

SHAIRA'S SECRET

'Ma, did you hear?' Shaira told her mother about the queen's lost necklace and the king's reward. She paused, before continuing. 'Ma, what if the crow dropped it at our home?'

Her mother smiled. 'Beti, stop dreaming. We have a lot of work to do. Here, dry these clothes.'

Shaira nodded, but did not move.

'Hurry, Shaira. Don't you want to buy some firecrackers?'

Shaira nodded then made her way home. She trudged down the road with an armful of wet clothes, drip, dripping on the grass and tears trickling down her face. What should she do about the necklace?

Finders keepers, losers weepers, a voice sang in Shaira's mind. But another voice cut in: *You did not earn it. It is not yours.* She knew Divaali celebrated the triumph of good over evil. How could she start the year by being dishonest? Ma would much prefer the pearls of honesty than the pearls of someone else's necklace.

Shaira went home, took her handkerchief with

the precious necklace wrapped in it, and headed for the king's palace. At the gates, the guards stopped her. 'I'm sorry, little girl, but you can't go into the palace.'

Shaira held up her little package. 'I have the queen's necklace.'

At once, the surprised guards led her up the steps and through the corridors to where the king and queen sat on their thrones.

Shaira bowed. 'Your Majesty, I have brought your necklace. A crow dropped it on my doorstep.' She untied the handkerchief and held up the seven-string pearl necklace.

The queen drew closer to examine the necklace. 'Yes!' she exclaimed. 'This is mine. Oh, sweet little girl — you found my necklace and you had the honesty to give it up!' She kissed Shaira on both cheeks and thanked her tearfully.

The queen's overflowing happiness made Shaira's eyes misty as well. She was glad she had returned the necklace. Ma would be proud of her.

The king presented Shaira a purse containing the reward money. 'Here, use it for whatever you want.'

But Shaira had something else in her mind and kindly declined the money.

The king and queen sat back, startled. 'What do you want, little girl? We'll give you whatever you desire,' said the king.

'Your Majesties,' Shaira hesitated. She knew the next day was the day of Lakshmi Puja. 'I want the whole city to be dark tomorrow.'

SHAIRA'S SECRET

The king frowned. 'What a strange request!'

But the queen said, 'A promise is a promise.'

And so the next day, the king's drummers and heralds proclaimed the decree as promised.

When night fell, Shaira took out every clay lamp she and her mother owned, filled them with oil and lit them. She arranged these sparkling divas in neat rows along each wall of their small home making sure there was not a single dark corner.

Outside, it was a quiet, moonless night. All the homes in the city, even the king's great marble palace, were hidden in darkness. Only Shaira's small house shone like a lone, bright star.

Suddenly, there were sounds of tinkling temple bells, followed by a knock on the door.

'Please let me in,' a gentle voice urged.

Shaira's mother looked wide-eyed. But Shaira smiled. 'Don't worry, Ma. We have a special guest.' She told the visitor, 'I will let you in only if you agree to bless us.'

'I will, I will,' replied the gentle voice.

Shaira ran to open the door.

A soft wind rushed in. And at the doorstep, Goddess Lakshmi glowed in a shimmering, pink silk sari covered with lotus flowers. On her head was a shiny, golden crown. She smiled at Shaira.

'The light of your divas drew me here,' she said. 'But the honesty in your heart shines with such radiance that I bless you.'

Shaira stood rooted to the earthen floor. She felt as if the light of all the divas in her home had lit up inside her.

The goddess admired the rangoli design on the doorstep. She picked up the pot of marigolds and it changed into a pot of gold coins. 'This pot will always be full,' she said, giving it to Shaira.

Shaira's trembling hands could hardly hold the heavy pot. She passed it to her mother. Now Ma would no longer have to be a washerwoman. That was the best Divaali gift of all.

Shaira and Ma both bent down to touch the feet of the goddess in reverence. 'Thank you, Goddess Lakshmi! Thank you for making this such a special Divaali!'

The goddess gave a radiant smile, and disappeared.

The night of Divaali, Shaira hurled the firecrackers into the air. The rockets exploded in the seven colours of the rainbow, just like the queen's seven-string pearl necklace. And she knew that from now on her whole world would be filled with these colours of joy.

83

KERALA

Kerala is known for its natural beauty, stretching from the Western Ghat Mountains to the sandy beaches, coconut groves and lush rainforests, like Kishkinda forest in 'Hanuman's Adventures'. Lanka, the stronghold of the demon king Ravana in the story, is the modern-day country of Sri Lanka, situated off the coast of Tamil Nadu.

The majority of people in Kerala are Hindus. Many of the teachings of Hinduism are included in the 'Ramayana', one of the two great Sanskrit epics of India. It is much shorter than the 'Mahabharata', though it is still very long — it fills seven books. The word 'Ramayana' literally means 'the march of Rama' and the story focuses on Rama, the prince of Ayodyha, who is sent into exile. When Ravana kidnaps Rama's wife, Sita, Rama searches all of India to find her. The story begins in northern India, and moves south as Rama searches for Sita. Hanuman is the monkey god that eventually helps Rama find Sita. Hanuman is worshipped as a symbol of physical strength, perseverance and devotion.

84

◆ The 'Ramayana' has been passed down through the generations in many forms — epic poems, folk tales, dance, music, puppet shows, paintings and even comic books, which are still found all over India.

◆ On Saturday and Tuesday, many Hindus fast in honour of Hanuman and give special offerings to him. It is common for Hindus to chant his name in times of trouble as a way of seeking protection.

◆ The festival of Dussehra celebrates Rama's triumph over the demon king Ravana. In Kerala, it is tradition that parents start the formal education of their children on the day of Dussehra.

◆ Kerala is known for being the most literate state in India.

◆ The Vilvamala Hill Temple in northern Kerala has two shrines — one dedicated to Rama and another dedicated to Lakshman, Rama's younger brother.

◆ The women of Kerala traditionally hold high status. Unlike elsewhere in India, family lineage and inheritance are passed down through the women of the family, rather than the men.

Hanuman's Adventures

Long ago when the demon Ravana tormented the world, the gods blessed the people with the birth of a supernatural monkey-boy. His name was Hanuman.

Hanuman was a happy little monkey who lived in the valley of trees in Kishkinda forest. He had a round, red face and a mischievous twinkle in his eye.

One day, Hanuman looked up at the sun and thought, *I will eat that ripe, golden fruit.* He flew into the sky and stretched out his arms to snatch it.

At once, the earth plunged into darkness. Hanuman's father, Pavana, the god of wind, came and pulled Hanuman on to his lap. 'Son, you are blessed with powers for a purpose,' he said. 'You should use them only to help others in distress.'

Hanuman let go of the sun and never forgot his father's words. Years passed and he grew as strong as a mountain and as tall as a tower. One morning, he awoke to see two mighty warriors armed with bows and arrows. Curious to find out more, he approached them and asked, 'What brings you here?'

The warriors looked up at the huge monkey-man in surprise.

'I am Rama, and this is my brother Lakshmana. We are the princes of Ayodyha.' Rama told Hanuman how he and his brother were forced to live in exile in the forest.

'We are looking for my wife, Sita,' said Rama. 'We came to you because we heard about your special powers.'

'Yesterday I saw a lady in Ravana's gold chariot. She dropped this.' Hanuman proudly showed a bangle that fitted one of his thick fingers like a ring.

'That is Sita's!' cried Rama. 'Ravana must have abducted her.'

'Ravana is our enemy too,' said Hanuman. 'He has killed many of my brothers and sisters in the forest. I will help you find Sita. Sit on my shoulders and I will give you a ride.' Rama climbed onto one of Hanuman's shoulders, Lakshmana climbed onto the other. Then Hanuman took one flying leap and landed in the valley of trees. He whistled and hundreds of monkeys hidden among the trees came out. They stared at Rama and Lakshmana.

KERALA

Hanuman told the monkeys, 'These men are our friends,' and he recounted Rama's tale.

'We shall search every corner of the forest until we find Sita!' cried the monkeys.

Hanuman took one flying leap and landed near the ocean. Searching along the seashore, he cried, 'Sita, Sita, Sita!' To the south, he saw the green island of Lanka floating like a jade jewel in the azure-blue water. Suddenly he spotted a diamond nose ring in the sand. Could it be Sita's? Hanuman took another flying leap back to Rama. 'Look what I found!'

'It is Sita's!' cried Rama. 'You also found her bangle. Sita must have deliberately dropped her jewellery to make a trail. Ravana must have taken Sita across the sea to the island of Lanka.' Rama looked up at Hanuman in despair. 'How can we get across the sea to Lanka?' he asked.

'I can easily hop over the sea. You wait here with my army of monkeys,' Hanuman said.

Rama agreed. Slipping off his signet ring, he gave it to Hanuman. 'Please give this ring to Sita. Tell her I will come and rescue her.'

Hanuman nodded and with one mighty leap, he flew into the sky. When he was halfway across to

HANUMAN'S ADVENTURES

Lanka, a huge sea monster with sharp fangs and hair that writhed like snakes jumped up.

'Stop!' screeched Surasa, the sea monster. 'I am Ravana's guardian.' With these words, she swallowed Hanuman in one big gulp.

Hanuman slipped down the monster's throat and landed in her cavernous stomach with a jolt. A vile stench hit him. Around him were the skeletons of other sea creatures that the monster had gobbled.

'Help!' Hanuman cried. *How will I get out?* he thought. Then he had an idea. Using his powers, he changed into a bee and began to sting Surasa.

'Ouch!' the sea monster screamed, doubling over in pain. 'Stop, please stop!'

But Hanuman did not stop. Finally, Surasa heaved and opened her mouth wide, and Hanuman flew out.

Quickly, he took a deep breath and his body began to grow tall and mighty into its usual giant size. Then he leapt into the air, stopping only when he landed on the island of Lanka.

Soon Hanuman came to a hill hidden among a thick grove of asoka trees. He could see a tall fortress on the hill that twinkled with lights. Taking a deep

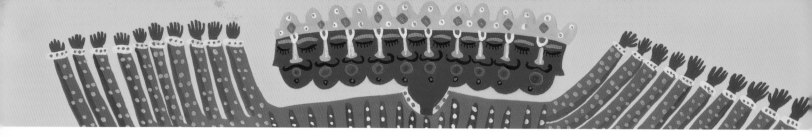

breath, he changed himself into a cat and crept inside the fortress. He checked every room, but could not find Sita. Then he heard a loud noise and followed it into a huge room. He froze. On a big golden bed, Ravana lay with his ten ugly heads and his ten sets of jaws open wide, snoring. But there was no Sita.

Hanuman wandered in the garden. There under an asoka tree, a woman in a white sari sat hugging her knees, crying. She was surrounded by demons, all fast asleep. In the light of the moon, Hanuman saw her face. It was so beautiful that he was sure the moon would hide in shame. *She must be Sita,* he thought. *She is exactly as Rama described her.* Slowly, he crept up to Sita's delicate feet and purred. She looked up at him in surprise.

'Please don't cry,' he said. 'I am Hanuman, the monkey-god. Lord Rama has sent me with his ring.'

Sita recognised the ring immediately and smiled through her tears. 'Is Rama well?'

Hanuman nodded just as a cry rang out in the darkness: 'Catch that talking black cat!'

Hanuman ran, but the guards caught him and took him to Ravana.

'Burn the wretched animal!' Ravana roared, furious to have been roused just for a silly cat.

So the guards grabbed Hanuman's tail, wrapped it in a rag dipped in oil and set it on fire. Hanuman used his powers to make his tail grow bigger and bigger. Puzzled, the guards kept on wrapping his tail

with more and more rags, but it kept growing.

Hanuman escaped. He ran all over the island spreading the fire, then one flying leap brought him back to the sea where he dipped his tail in the cool water. He prayed to the gods to keep Sita safe and swore to return with Rama to save her. Taking a deep breath, he grew back to his giant size, and leapt back to the mainland where Rama waited patiently.

'Sita is well,' Hanuman told Rama. 'But she's a prisoner of Ravana guarded by hundreds of demons.'

Meanwhile on Lanka, Ravana and his demon guards used every container they had to carry water from the sea to put out the great fire. By the time the fire was out, they had used up nearly all the sea water and could see the ocean floor.

Back in the forest, Hanuman and Rama watched the level of the sea recede further and further and were overjoyed. Surasa, the sea monster, would die without water. They made a plan to attack Ravana.

Hanuman and the monkeys rolled boulders and dropped them into what was left of the sea until they had built a long bridge that stretched all the way to Lanka. Finally, the march to the island began.

Ravana laughed when he heard about Hanuman, Rama and the approaching monkeys. 'Foolish Rama! We'll win this battle in the blink of an eye!'

The drums rolled and the battle of Lanka began. What a fierce battle it was! Rama and his brother Lakshmana, both skilful archers, shot their

KERALA

arrows, killing hundreds of demons, while Hanuman and his army of monkeys picked up rocks and trees and hurled them at their enemies.

Soon it was clear that Rama and the monkeys were winning the war. Fuming, Ravana entered the battlefield. 'I will kill Rama myself.' He towered before Rama like an enormous volcano about to erupt, as flames leapt out of his ten noses and smoke billowed out of his twenty ears.

Hanuman knelt down and let Rama climb on to his shoulder. Ravana laughed. He whipped his twenty arms into a whirlwind.

Rama fired a rush of fiery arrows that hit Ravana's heads, but as soon as one of his heads fell, another appeared in its place.

Hanuman looked up at Rama and whispered in his ear. Rama nodded, took aim and shot his last arrow. It arched in the sky like Lord Indra's thunderbolt and hit Ravana's navel. Suddenly, Ravana exploded into a ball of fire. The demon was dead.

Everyone cheered as Hanuman led Rama to the garden where Sita was waiting. Overjoyed, Rama and Sita hugged each other, crying tears of joy, then turned to thank Hanuman and his monkeys. Rama reached out and held Hanuman's big paw. 'I am Vishnu, the Lord of Creation. I have come to Earth in the body of a prince to fight evil. I will never forget what you did for us.'

Sources

India – general

◆ *DK Eyewitness Travel Guides: India*. Dorling Kindersley, London. 2002.

◆ Seth, Kailash N. *Gods and Goddesses of India*. Diamond Pocket Books Pvt. Ltd, New Delhi. 1999.

Andhra Pradesh

◆ 'Andhra Pradesh'. Answers.com. *The Columbia Electronic Encyclopedia, Sixth Edition*, Columbia University Press. 2003. http://www.answers.com/topic /andhra-pradesh, accessed 5 January 2006.

◆ 'Andhra Pradesh'. Encyclopædia Britannica Premium Service. http://www.britannica.com/eb/article? tocId=46305, accessed 21 December 2005.

◆ Andhra Pradesh, 'The Kohinoor of India', www.aptourism.com, accessed 20 December 2005.

◆ Delhi Tourism, 'Classical Dance 'Kuchipudi' from Andhra Pradesh', http://www.delhitourism.com/dance/, accessed 21 December 2005.

◆ Indiasite, 'Andhra Pradesh Tourism', www.indiasite.com/andhrapradesh/, accessed 21 December 2005.

Gujarat

◆ Jain, Rashimi, 'Mehendi Wedding Customs', http://www.mehendiworld.com/mehendi-wedding-customs.htm, accessed 14 February 2006.

◆ Official Portal of Gujarat Government, 'Gujarat Tourism', http://www.gujaratindia.com/VisitGujarat/ VisitGujarat7.htm, accessed 29 November 2005.

◆ Places of Peace and Power, 'Dwarka, India', http://www.sacredsites.com/asia/india/dwarka.html, accessed 29 November 2005.

◆ Vibrant Gujarat, 'Fairs and Festivals', http://www.gujarattourism.com/festivals/index.html, accessed 29 November 2005.

Kerala

◆ Das, Subhamoy, 'Hanuman: Simian Symbol of Strength', http://hinduism.about.com/library/weekly/ aa052801a.htm, accessed 28 December 2005.

◆ Incredible India, 'Kerala', http://www.tourismofindia.com/sts/stkerala.htm, accessed 28 December 2005.

◆ Kerala Tourism, 'Travel Zone', http://www.keralatourism.org/, accessed 22 December 2005.

◆ Kerala, 'Ramayana', http://www.keralaonline.com/ dailydose/spirituality/display.asp?cap=ramayana.htm, accessed 22 December 2005.

◆ Kerala, PBS.org, 'Hidden India: The Kerala Spicelands', http://www.pbs.org/hiddenindia/religion/, accessed 28 December 2005.

◆ Kerala. Answers.com. *The Columbia Electronic Encyclopedia, Sixth Edition*, Columbia University Press, 2003. http://www.answers.com/topic/kerala, accessed 29 March 2006.

◆ Ramayana, 'Temples of Kerala', http://www.templenet.com/Kerala/kerala_ramayana.html, accessed 22 December 2005.

◆ Ramayana. Answers.com. *The Columbia Electronic Encyclopedia, Sixth Edition*, Columbia University Press, 2003. http://www.answers.com/topic/ramayana, accessed 28 December 2005.

◆ Religion Facts, 'The Ramayana', http://www.religionfacts.com/hinduism/texts/ ramayana.htm, accessed 28 December 2005.

◆ Tiruvilvamala, 'Temples of Kerala', http://www.templenet.com/Kerala/tiruvilvamala.html, accessed 28 December 2005.

Nagaland

◆ Himalayan Kingdoms, 'Nagaland: General Information', http://www.himalayankingdoms.com/destinationinfo .ihtml?destid=29, accessed 29 November 2005.

◆ Himalayan Mercantile, 'Naga Artifacts', http://www.himalayan-mercantile.com/nagaland/ hmn55.html, accessed 21 February 2006.

◆ Incredible India, 'Places to Visit: Nagaland', http://www.incredibleindia.org/newsite/ cms_Page.asp?pageid=384, accessed 14 February 2006.

◆ Kalla, Avinash, 'The Land of the Nagas', http://www.the-south-asian.com/June2004/nagas.htm, accessed 29 November 2005.

◆ Nagaland, 'Dress and Ornaments', http://www.webindia123.com/nagaland/People/ dresornam.htm, accessed 21 February 2006.

◆ North East India Travel, 'Nagaland Travel', http://www.northeastindiadiary.com/nagaland-travel/, accessed 29 November 2005.

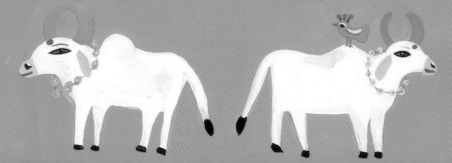

◆ Pye, Michael and Elliot Shaw, eds. 'Tribal Religions of India', *Overview of World Religions*, http://philtar.ucsm.ac.uk/encyclopedia/india/tribal.html, accessed 21 February 2006.

Punjab

◆ 'Indian Cuisine', *Travel and Living*, Discovery Communications, Inc, http://www.travelandliving.co.uk/food/indian_cuisine/punjab/index.shtml, accessed 2 December 2005.

◆ 'Punjab da platter', *The Hindu Times*, http://www.hindu.com/thehindu/mp/2004/06/30/stories/2004063000280400.htm, accessed 2 December 2005.

◆ 'Punjab', Answers.com. *The Columbia Electronic Encyclopedia, Sixth Edition*, Columbia University Press, 2003. http://www.answers.com/topic/punjab, accessed 2 December 2005.

◆ Cookery: Regional Special Recipes, 'Punjabi Dishes', http://www.webindia123.com/cookery/region/punjab/intro.htm, accessed 2 December 2005.

◆ India Heritage, 'Punjabi Cuisine', http://www.indiaheritage.org/cuisine/cuisine_type.php?type=Punjabi, accessed 2 December 2005.

◆ Nath, Dr. V. 'The Contribution of Punjab to India's Cultural Mosaic', *The Sikh Review*. http://www.sikhreview.org/july2002/heritage.htm, accessed 2 December 2005.

◆ Punjab, 'Culture and History', http://punjabgovt.nic.in/CULTURE/SocietyCulture.htm, accessed 1 December 2005.

◆ Punjab, 'Early History', http://thegreatindian.tripod.com/panjabState/punjab.htm, accessed 20 December 2005.

◆ Saran, Suvin. 'Regional Cooking', http://www.suvir.com/regionalcooking.html, accessed 2 December 2005.

◆ Wedding Rituals, 'Punjabi Weddings', http://www.shaadi.com/wedding/rituals/wedding/040305-punjabi-wed.php, accessed 21 December 2005.

Rajasthan

◆ Dances of Rajasthan, 'Ghoomar Dance', http://www.indiasite.com/rajasthan/jaipur/dances.html, accessed 29 November 2005.

◆ Gluckman, Ron. 'Live Like a King in the Castles of Rajasthan', *Time Asia*.

http://rajasthantourism.gov.in/rajasthan/Article/articles.htm, accessed 30 November 2005.

◆ Government of Rajasthan, 'History of Rajasthan', http://www.rajasthan.gov.in/History.SHTM, accessed 1 December 2005.

◆ Government of Rajasthan, 'Travel and Tourism', http://www.rajasthantourism.gov.in/, accessed 29 November 2005.

◆ India Hills, 'Rajasthan', http://www.indyahills.com/raj/raj.htm, accessed 1 December 2005.

◆ Rajasthan, 'Travel Guide', http://www.rajasthanindia.co.uk/, accessed 30 November 2005.

◆ Rajasthan, 'Udaipur & Jaipur', http://www.fodors.com/miniguides/mgresults.cfm?destination=rajasthan@216&cur_section=ove, accessed 30 November 2005.

◆ Tourism in Rajasthan, 'About Rajasthan', http://www.tourisminrajasthan.com/rajasthan-travel-guide/about-rajasthan.html, accessed 29 November 2005.

Tamil Nadu

◆ 'Tamil Nadu'. Answers.com. *The Columbia Electronic Encyclopedia, Sixth Edition*, Columbia University Press, 2003. http://www.answers.com/topic/tamil-nadu, accessed 6 December 2005.

◆ Tamil Nadu Tourism, 'Temples', http://www.tamilnadutourism.org/, accessed 17 October 2005.

◆ Tamil Nadu, 'Introduction', http://www.cs.utk.edu/~siddhart/tamilnadu/, accessed 17 October 2005.

Uttar Pradesh

◆ 'Uttar Pradesh'. Encyclopædia Britannica. 2005. Encyclopædia Britannica Online. http://www.search.eb.com/eb/article-46103, accessed 17 October 2005.

◆ India Profile, 'Taj Mahal, Agra', http://www.indiaprofile.com/monuments-temples/tajmahal.htm, accessed 6 December 2005.

◆ Taj Mahal, 'Visiting the Taj Mahal', http://www.pbs.org/treasuresoftheworld/taj_mahal/tlevel_1/t4_visiting.html, accessed 6 December 2005.

To all the children of the world — S. N.

For my mother, Eileen — C. C.

The author would like to express her gratitude to
Tessa Strickland & Kim Duncan-Mooney at Barefoot;
Karyn Henley, Katya Simpson, Sheleza Manji, Nargis Rawji, Sippy Chinna,
Shiraz Kurji; and her family — Astrum, Shaira & Mohamed Nanji.

Barefoot Books
124 Walcot Street
Bath BA1 5BG

This book has been printed on 100% acid-free paper

Graphic design by Katie Stephens, Bristol
Colour separation by Bright Arts, Singapore
Printed and bound in China by Printplus, Ltd

This book was typeset in Catull, Cronos and Bembo
The illustrations were prepared in gouache on Fabriano paper

Paperback ISBN 978-1-84686-426-1

British Cataloguing-in-Publication Data:
a catalogue record for this book is available from the British Library

1 3 5 7 9 8 6 4 2